This Notebook Belongs To :

....

....

Published By
Semoni Printing Pro

Date: .... / .... / ....

Date: .... / .... / ....

Date: .... / .... / ....

Date: .... / .... / ....

Date: .... / .... / ....

Date: .... / .... / ....

Date: .... /........ /...............

Date: .... / .... / ....

Date: .... / .... / ....

Date: .... / .... / ....

Date: .... / .... / ....

Date: .... / .... / ....

Date: .... / .... / ....

Date: .... / .... / ....

Date: .... / .... / ....

Date: .... / .... / ....

Date: .... /........ /..............

Date: .... / .... / ....

Date: .... / .... / ....

Date: .... /........ /.............

Date: .... / .... / ....

Date: .... /........ /..............

Date: .... /........ /..............

Date: .... / .... / ....

Date: .... /........ /..............

Date: .... /........ /..............

Date: .... /........ /..............

Date: .... / .... / ....

Date: .... / .... / ....

Date: .... / .... / ....

Date: .... /........ /..............

Date: .... /........ /..............

Date: .... /........ /..............

Date: .... / .... / ....

Date: .... / .... / ....

Date: .... / .... / ....

Date: .... / .... / ....

Date: .... / .... / ....

Date: .... / .... / ....

Date: .... / .... / ....

Date: .... / .... / ....

Date: .... / .... / ....

Date: .... / .... / ....

Date: .... /........ /..............

Date: .... /........ /..............

Date: .... /........ /..............

Date: .... / .... / ....

Date: .... /........ /...............

Date: .... / .... / ....

Date: .... / .... / ....

Date: .... /........ /.............

Date: .... / .... / ....

Date: .... / .... / ....

Date: .... /........ /...............

Date: .... / .... / ....

Date: .... / .... / ....

Date: .... / .... / ....

Date: .... / .... / ....

Date: .... / .... / ....

Date: .... / .... / ....

Date: .... / .... / ....

Date: .... / .... / ....

Date: .... /........ /..............

Date: .... / .... / ....

Date: .... / .... / ....

Date: .... / .... / ....

Date: .... / .... / ....

Date: .... /........ /..............

Date: .... / .... / ....

Date: .... /........ /..............

Date: .... / .... / ....

Date: .... / .... / ....

Date: .... / .... / ....

Date: .... /........ /..............

Date: .... /........ /..............

Date: .... / .... / ....

Date: .... / .... / ....

Date: .... / .... / ....

Date: .... / .... / ....

Date: .... / .... / ....

Date: .... /........ /.............

Date: .... /........ /..............

Date: .... / .... / ....

Date: .... / .... / ....

Date: .... /........ /..............

Date: .... / .... / ....

Date: .... / .... / ....

Date: .... / .... / ....

Date: .... /........ /..............

Date: .... / .... / ....

Date: .... /........ /..............

Date: .... /........ /..............

Date: .... / .... / ....

Date: .... / .... / ....

Date: .... / .... / ....

Date: .... /........ /..............

Finish.

Made in the USA
Monee, IL
20 December 2021

86644289R10059